BOOK ANALYSIS

By Benjamin Taylor

Tinker Tailor Soldier Spy

BY JOHN LE CARRÉ

Bright
≡Summaries.com

JOHN LE CARRÉ

ENGLISH NOVELIST

- **Born in Dorset (England) in 1931.**
- **Notable works:**
  - *The Spy Who Came in from the Cold* (1963), novel
  - *The Night Manager* (1993), novel
  - *The Constant Gardener* (2001), novel

John le Carré, born in Dorset, England in 1931 as David Cornwell, is an internationally renowned writer of espionage novels and short stories. After studying at the University of Oxford and enjoying a brief teaching career, le Carré was employed by the British Foreign Service in West Berlin, where he learnt many of the informed details about espionage and international relations that are found throughout his works. While working for MI5 and MI6, le Carré began writing, and launched a career as a novelist spanning over 50 years and dozens of books with his first work, *Call for the Dead* (1961). His first successful novel was *The Spy Who Came in from the Cold* (1963), which was an internationally acclaimed bestseller. His espionage novels are often set during the Cold War and feature British intelligence agents in a more bureaucratic and realistic light, compared with the traditional glamorisation of spies in popular fiction. Many of his books and stories have been successfully adapted for the cinema and television, and he is now one of the most well-respected and celebrated English novelists of the postwar period.

TINKER TAILOR SOLDIER SPY

SPYING ON THE SPIES

- **Genre:** novel
- **Reference edition:** Le Carré, J. (2017) *Tinker Tailor Soldier Spy*. London: Sceptre.
- **1ˢᵗ edition:** 1974
- **Themes:** war, nostalgia, espionage, Britain, double agents, Empire, Soviet Union

Published in 1974 and set in the previous year, *Tinker Tailor Soldier Spy* is the first of a trilogy of le Carré novels known as *The Karla Trilogy*, which feature the character of the retired English spy George Smiley and his nemesis, the Russian spymaster Karla. Smiley is a character who appears throughout le Carré's work, including in his very first novel *The Spy Who Came in from the Cold*. The plot of *Tinker Tailor Soldier Spy*, which details the rooting out of a mole in the British Intelligence Service (known fictionally as the Circus), is said to draw from real-life British double agents during the Second World War and the first stages of the Cold War labelled the Cambridge Five (called so because they had been recruited out of the University of Cambridge), who covertly supplied sensitive information to the Soviet Union. The novel is well-regarded and critically acclaimed for its realistic portrayal of the world of espionage, and was made into a feature-length film in 2011 starring Gary Oldman, Colin Firth and Benedict Cumberbatch.

SUMMARY

OUT OF RETIREMENT

George Smiley, a retired agent for the British Intelligence Service – known as the Circus – is approached by Peter Guillam, an old colleague and the head of a department called the 'scalphunters', which deals with assassinations too conspicuous for overseas agents. He tells Smiley that there is rumoured to be a spy deep in the heart of the Circus known as Gerald, planted by Karla, the mysterious head of the Moscow Centre. This information was unearthed by Ricki Tarr, a disgraced agent who came across a Soviet defector. Smiley and the former head of the Circus, Control, were forced to retire from their roles after a disastrous mission in Czechoslovakia during which Jim Prideaux, then an agent, was shot and captured by the Soviets. This mission, codenamed Operation Testify, had also been following Control's suspicions of there being a mole within the Circus. Smiley chooses to confront the past and agrees to help Guillam discover the identity of the mole.

Smiley returns to Oxford, where he went to university, and talks to Camilla, a former researcher for the Circus, about Polyakov, a Soviet diplomat working out of London who she strongly suspected of espionage in the 60s, but who she was eventually told not to investigate by the new head of the Circus, Percy Alleline. Polyakov was trained by Karla, and Smiley suspects that he has links with the mole in the Circus.

INVESTIGATIONS

Smiley makes the Hotel Islay in Sussex Gardens his base of operations, getting Guillam to steal and drop off information to him in his investigations. In particular, he gets him to provide him with intelligence relating to Operation Witchcraft, a high-profile intelligence gathering operation organised by Alleline (who at the time was rising through the ranks), from a source labelled 'Merlin', as well as any information on Prideaux and the circumstances surrounding Operation Testify. Smiley reads of Control's resentment of Alleline, a careerist and an untrustworthy man who eventually replaced him as head of the Circus. He details the suspiciously invaluable nature of the reports Alleline was producing via his contact 'Merlin' and how the importance of the reports seemed to raise Alleline's profile within the Circus, leaving out Control, who became more and more distrusting of Alleline and his colleagues around him.

Eventually, the Witchcraft operation was given a special committee, made up of Alleline and three others: Roy Bland, Toby Esterhase and Bill Haydon – who is Smiley's wife's cousin with whom she had an affair. Smiley describes the slow deposition of Control as head of the Circus, and the suspicious nature of Witchcraft and Merlin. He finds that after Control's death, the reports concerning Merlin changed dramatically – most significantly detailing his being given a house in London through which to work. Just after making this discovery, Smiley receives a phone call from a worried Guillam. The files on Operation Testify had been more difficult to acquire, and Guillam must steal the files from the Circus archives, which is an incredibly dangerous task. He is just about to succeed when Esterhase corners him and tells him that Alleline needs his help with something.

INCREASING DANGER

Alleline questions Guillam about Ricki Tarr, who he labels a defector – and who it is illegal for Guillam to contact. Guillam falsely claims not to have talked to him and is allowed to leave. He and Smiley question Tarr and find that he had failed to tell them that he has arranged for his wife and children to travel to England, alerting the Circus to his presence. Afterwards, they go to a restaurant and Smiley tells Guillam about the time he met Karla and attempted to get him to defect. Later that night, while poring over research, Smiley realises that Polyakov is an emissary between the mole, Gerald and the source Merlin, passing useless Soviet 'secrets' as reports to the British, and providing the Soviets with valuable British information – using the London property as a safe house.

Smiley visits Sam, a bookie and the duty manager at the Circus the night Jim Prideaux was shot, to fill in details he finds have been taken out of the Operation Testify file. He learns that Alleline came soon after the news of the botched mission broke to take over, and that Bill Haydon suspiciously knew about the mission but not that an agent had been shot. Smiley continues his investigation, interviewing Max, who was Jim Prideaux's bodyguard in Czechoslovakia during Operation Testify. He reads about Prideaux and Bill Haydon, who were friends at university before the war and whose relationship, it seems, went beyond mere friendship at times. Finally, he goes to see an old friend, Jerry Westerby, who tells Smiley that he heard a story about Operation Testify, according to which the Soviets knew all about the operation before it even happened.

Smiley goes to see Jim Prideaux at the boys' school where he works. Jim is irritable, haunted by his past and seems to have been abandoned by the Circus since Operation Testify. Jim reveals that the real reason behind Testify was Control attempting to find the name of the mole in the Circus. The mission was a trap as the Czechs knew he was coming, and he was captured and interrogated. Jim reveals that Karla interrogated him at one point and asked about Smiley. Jim revealed the real nature of Testify to him and was eventually let go. He claims that on returning home, after weeks of waiting, Toby Esterhase came to him and told him to forget everything.

THE MOLE REVEALED

Smiley and Guillam go to see Toby Esterhase and, after telling him what they know, get him to reveal the location of the London safe house where Polyakov and Gerald meet to pass information to and from the Soviet Union. In order to draw out Gerald, Smiley asks Ricki Tarr to send out a coded message to Alleline telling him that he has highly important information – which would spark a meeting between Gerald (who would have intercepted the message) and Polyakov. It works, and Bill Haydon arrives at the safe house; he is revealed to be the mole and to have betrayed them. Smiley discovers from Bill that he turned to the Soviets due to Britain's diminishing influence in the world, and because of his dislike of America. Bill is found dead soon after talking to Smiley at the house in which he is imprisoned, though they do not know who killed him.

CHARACTER STUDY

GEORGE SMILEY

George Smiley, a recurring character in le Carré's novels, is a former agent for the Circus, one of the 'old guard' recruited in the build-up to the Second World War (1939-45). He is forced into retirement after the disastrous fallout from Operation Testify. He is described as "small, podgy and at best middle-aged, he was by experience one of London's meek who do not inherit the earth" (p. 20), and "a shy man, for all his vanities, and one who expected very little communication" (p. 229). He is haunted and angered by the past, his professional and personal failures, and the enemies he feels he has made along the way. Because of this, he spends his retirement pursuing "the profession of forgetting" (p. 87). He is therefore hesitant, when approached by Guillam for help, at the idea of re-opening the events of the past and facing up to the source of his resentments. Due to the nature of his investigations, the past and present seem to merge together at times for him, and he reflects that "at a certain moment after all, every man chooses: will he go forward, will he go back" (p. 29). Though Smiley must address his past during his mission, the novel essentially follows Smiley's choosing the former: settling old suspicions so he can move on from his past.

Smiley thinks often of his wife, Ann, who is described as "the last illusion of an illusionless man" (p. 416) – an encouraging piece of irrationality in an almost exclusively rational and practical man. Though she is notoriously unfaithful to him and they are separated during the book, he is still clearly in love with her and often reminisces about her and the mistakes he has made in their relationship. She represents the intertwining of his personal and professional life due to the well-publicised affair that she has with Bill Haydon (who it is later revealed plotted the whole thing).

BILL HAYDON

Bill Haydon is of the same generation as George, recruited by the Circus before the war and described by Guillam as "one of the unrepeatable, fading Circus generation, to which his parents and George Smiley also belonged" (p. 99). He is "ubiquitous and charming, unorthodox and occasionally outrageous" (p. 177), the cousin and lover of Smiley's wife, Ann, and old school friend of Jim Prideaux, with whom it is implied he had a romantic relationship. At the start of the novel, Bill is a high-ranking official within the Circus and one of the architects of Operation Witchcraft, along with Alleline, Bland and Esterhase. Smiley's investigations reveal him to be the mole, Gerald, who is passing sensitive information directly to the Soviet Union via the diplomat Polyakov.

He reveals the reasons behind his betrayal to Smiley at the end of the novel. He was essentially trained with the pretensions of England as a world power, expecting to covertly guide the shaping of the world through England's standing. However, he is disillusioned by the collapse of the British Empire after the Second World War and rise of America and the Soviet Union. As Smiley claims of his actions, he was: "an ambitious man born to the big canvas, brought up to rule, divide and conquer, whose visions and vanities were fixed [...] on the world game" (p. 394). Haydon is representative of the enduring and outdated notions of England's importance in the world at the time – turning to the Soviet Union when he realises that his ambition cannot be fulfilled working in Britain

JIM PRIDEAUX

Also known by the professional pseudonym 'Jim Ellis', Jim and the precariousness of his lifestyle are the remnants of the fallout from the disastrous Operation Testify. He was shot twice in the back during the mission, then tortured and interrogated by the Soviets before being sent back to England. During the novel, he is working as a substitute teacher for a boys' prep school and lives with the same attitude to the past as George Smiley – resolutely trying to forget old and unsettled betrayals and suspicions yet failing miserably to do so. He was recruited for the Circus by Bill Haydon, his old friend from Oxford, and possible lover. He is described as having an "aura of gentleness that surrounded him, a gentleness only possible in big men seen through the eyes of boys" (p. 13). He is physical, eccentric and resolutely patriotic, with a "passionate Englishness [...] England was his love; when it came down to it, no one suffered for her" (*ibid.*).

KARLA

Like Smiley, Karla is a recurring character in le Carré's novels, as the head of the Moscow Centre and foil to his protagonist. He is a mysterious and often unseen character in the novel, only recollected once by Smiley, who interrogated him long ago without knowing then who he was: "legends were made, and Karla was one of them. Even his age was a mystery [...] Decades of his life were not accounted for and probably never would be" (p. 228). He is, however, a prominent figure in the background of *Tinker Tailor Soldier Spy*, described as a "little wiry chap, with silvery hair, bright brown eyes and plenty of wrinkles [...] tough, whatever that means and sagacious within the limits of his experience" (p. 235). He is Smiley's nemesis, and acts as the Soviet puppet master in the novel, with a vast network of spies including Bill Haydon, whose betrayal acts as the central plot device. His and Smiley's relationship seems to represent the senseless and intransigent nature of the Cold War as a conflict. Smiley addresses this when they speak in India during an interrogation: "we've spent our lives looking for weaknesses in each other's systems. I can see through Eastern values just as you can see through Western ones [...] Don't you think it's time to recognise that there is as little worth on your side as there is on mine?" (p. 243).

ANALYSIS

HISTORICAL CONTEXT

Tinker Tailor Soldier Spy is set in 1973, a time of significant turbulence in the world in terms of international relations. Following the Second World War, the USA and the USSR emerged as the major powers, and their bitter economic, political and ideological rivalries caused the Cold War, a 30-year-long nuclear stalemate between the two superpowers and their various allies. Due to the devastating prospect of a nuclear war between the two, agitation was often either tentative or covert, with vast spying networks set up and exploited around the world. This is the world of *Tinker Tailor Soldier Spy*, one of fear, suspicion and the constant looming threat of annihilatory nuclear war.

At the heart of the conflict between these two nations is the basic systematic clash between the Capitalist West, with America as its figurehead, and the Communist Soviet Union. This ideological contrast had raged zealously throughout the world during the first half of the 20th century and was a contributing factor to the outbreak of the Second World War. Following the war, having liberated countries like Poland, Czechoslovakia and Hungary in Eastern Europe from German occupation, the Soviet Union set about instituting Communist rule. This met with ideological resistance from the USA and many Western Capitalist societies naturally aligned with it – a division represented by the splitting of Berlin into East and West with the Berlin Wall. The USSR spent the subsequent decades attempting to maintain and consolidate its influence in Europe and Asia. Meanwhile, the USA was attempting to stem the tide of Socialist thought, notably by entering into the Vietnam War (1964-75) in an attempt to prevent the Communist North Vietnam from bringing its southern neighbour under its control. Roy Bland jokes of the ideological differences to Smiley early in the novel: "As a good Socialist I'm going for the money. As a good capitalist I'm sticking with the revolution, because if you can't beat it spy on it" (p. 174).

BRITAIN'S DECLINE ON THE WORLD STAGE

Following the Second World War, Britain entered a period of steady decolonisation, losing a vast number of its many overseas territories, including India (1947), Burma (1948) and all of its African colonies. This, and the emergence of the USA and the Soviet Union as world superpowers, meant that Britain at the time of the novel is a country of fading influence and power, with the ghost of the British Empire serving as a constant reminder of past supremacy. Indeed, much of the novel is concerned with the changing identity and impotence of Britain, particularly noticeable amongst the old generation of the likes of George Smiley and Bill Haydon, who are old enough to have served the British Empire at the height of its power: "trained to empire, trained to rule the waves. All gone. All taken away" (p. 129). They are anachronisms, trained to be the secret stalwarts of an empire that, by 1973, no longer exists.

Indeed, Bill Haydon, who is described as "the torchbearer of a certain kind of antiquated romanticism – a notion of English calling" (p. 396), turns to the Soviet Union because of this very diminishing power. He, and many others like him, were brought up with the idea of Britain as a supreme power, only to find that power swiftly draining away. He cites the Suez Crisis (1956), during which the Egyptian President Gabel Abdel Nassar seized control of the Suez Canal – which had been owned by British and French concerns – as the final straw that turned him to betrayal, having "finally persuaded him of the inanity of the British situation and of the British capacity to spike the advance of history while not being able to offer anything in terms of contribution" (p. 411). Amongst the monumental struggle of the Cold War, Britain in 1973 was a place realising the extent of its impotence.

PARANOIA AND THE LIFE OF A SPY

With this novel set in and around the central British Intelligence Service, the Circus, le Carré presents a world of suspicion, paranoia and fear, and shows the life of a spy to be one of constant agitation and disquiet, far from the glamour and heroism of traditional fictional portrayals of spies. George Smiley in particular is constantly worrying about his past affecting his present and talks of "the secret fear that follows every professional to his grave. Namely, that one day, out of a past so complex that even he could not remember all the enemies he might have made, one of them would find him and demand the reckoning" (p. 30). Throughout the Circus, suspicion is rife, and it is a place where even close friends are seemingly unable to trust each other. It is a testament to the secrecy and paranoia of the Cold War years, during which everyone could be suspected, that a mole right at the heart of an intelligence organisation is almost to be expected: "We always accepted that sooner or later it would happen. We always warned one another: be on your guard. We've turned enough members of other outfits" (p. 324). This atmosphere of paranoia is exacerbated by the agents' understanding of the moral ambivalence of their situation – many of them addressing the fact that, due to the complexity of the political tensions during the Cold War, there is no morally right or wrong side. As Jim Prideaux remarks of the life of an agent: "survival [...] is an infinite capacity for suspicion" (p. 374).

THE MODERN WORLD AND A FADING GENERATION

Along with the drastic social changes that forced Britain to re-evaluate its identity, in the years following the Second World War, new technologies had a hugely transformative effect on all aspects of societies around the world. References to this strange new world are ubiquitous in *Tinker Tailor Soldier Spy*, particularly by the fading older war generation through which much of the narrative is told. For example, George Smiley is often irritated and anxious about the modern world and is on the brink of upping sticks and moving to the countryside when he is contacted by Peter Guillam. The rapid transformation of the previous 25 years can be seen even in the most mundane aspects of his life, such as his home: "When he had first come to live here these Georgian cottages had a modest, down-at-heel charm with young couples making do on fifteen pounds a week and a tax-free lodger hidden in the basement. Now steel screens protected their lower windows and for each house three cars jammed in the back" (pp. 29-30). The society depicted in this quote is one that is clearly less community-driven and more overtly consume-rist, and Smiley and those of his generation's growing disaffection with the world around them is a running theme throughout the novel.

FURTHER REFLECTION

SOME QUESTIONS TO THINK ABOUT...

- How does le Carré invoke the atmosphere of the Cold War? Do you think this presentation is realistic?
- How might le Carré's work have been influenced by his time working for the British Intelligence Service? How does this insight into the world of espionage affect the novel?
- Compare George Smiley and his fellow agents to other fictional spies in popular culture. How, for example, does Smiley compare to James Bond?
- The relationship between George Smiley and his nemesis Karla is played out over several of le Carré's books. Does this add to or take away from the novel in any way?
- The Second World War had a major effect on the world in the second half of the 20th century. What remnants from the war can be seen in *Tinker Tailor Soldier Spy*? Did it have any positive effects?

- How does the novel compare to the film adaptation? Think about how you might go about adapting the book for the screen or stage.
- Consider le Carré's attitudes toward Britain and its place in the world in the novel. 40 years after it was published, how has Britain's identity changed or stayed the same in the context of international relations? What remnants of the Cold War can we see around us in the world today?

We want to hear from you!
Leave a comment on your online library
and share your favourite books on social media!

FURTHER READING

REFERENCE EDITION

- le Carré, J. (2017) *Tinker Tailor Soldier Spy*. London: Sceptre.

ADAPTATIONS

- *Tinker Tailor Soldier Spy*. (2011) [Film]. Tomas Alfredson. Dir. UK/France: StudioCanal and Working Title Films.

www.brightsummaries.com

Ebook EAN: 9782808015752

Paperback EAN: 9782808015769

Legal Deposit: D/2018/12603/546

Cover: © Primento

Digital conception by Primento, the digital partner of
publishers.

Printed in Great Britain
by Amazon

53646526R10029